Sam - Thank You!

Breathing

Through

Concrete

'Breathing' is essential, allow these characters to fulfill the passion of their lives into your heart.

Ameerah

2020

Copyright © 2019 Ameerah Shabazz-Bilal

All rights reserved. No part of this publication may be reproduced, distributed, or transmitted in any form or by any means, including photocopying, recording, or other electronic or mechanical methods, without the prior written permission of the publisher, except in the case of brief quotations embodied in critical reviews and certain other noncommercial uses permitted by copyright law. For permission requests, write to the publisher, addressed "Attention: Permissions Coordinator," at the address below.

ISBN: 978-1-7324557-4-0

LCCN: 2020905544

Published by Rebel Ink Publishing

Designed by Ras Heru Stewart

DEDICATION

To my Mother...

Carolanne Georgette Harris-McBride, who gifted me life through the infinite mercy of Allah, the creator of All Things.

Birthing me here on the very day of her own 16th birthday. Young, strong, unyielding, beautiful, wise, and fiery.

You made me strong. I am forever grateful.
I cannot just love a memory; I love you,

forever.

FOREWORD

By David Roberts (a.k.a. D-Black)

HOPE is the word that comes to mind whenever coming in contact with Sister Ameerah's work. She gives you the concrete, the rose, the plant, the soil. The beautiful and the gritty. But in the midst of all that is given, you will walk away elevated. Each line is crafted as true storytelling. You will experience the feelings, the thoughts, the struggles, and the triumphs that many of us are thankful for as we go through our journey called life.

Your eyes and mind will thank you for embracing this treat. Whether you're reading about the future royalty of our current generation or celebrating the life of someone who has cleaned up her or his life, each word is a joy. Every stanza is heroic.

"Sister Ameerah please take your place on this mantle. Bask in your work. Receive the radiance that you have sent out to the world, ten-fold.

Thank you for your excellence, love, and care, and for showcasing the humanity in all of us."

A Note from Dr. Zain Abdullah

Words sear her pages then take flight. Ameerah Shabazz captures pain, hope, more pain, and even the yearning of desire. A good poet can make us grasp life's journey. A great poet makes us experience it again and again. This beautiful book of poetry makes me experience life anew.

TABLE OF CONTENTS

Apnea (prologue)

I know this Tongue Gives Life

The Block

Seconds Clean

Angel Down

They Speak to My Soul

Open Windows

I Just Called to Say I Love You…

Broken Child

Our Streets

Dear Broken Girl

I Promised Her

She is Beautiful...

His Shoes

Polyptotons

Breathing...

Beautiful Naturally

Fires of Memories

Reflect

Grateful

Crevices

Breathing and Hoping for Wind

Inhale

Exhale

Breathing

The Ashes

Do inhaling

and exhaling

define life?

Apnea (Prologue)

The first cry...

the labored intake of air entering the lungs of life

for the first time.

To breathe.

Allowing that warm gaping breath to exit,
not knowing fear or futures...

breathing which allows the hard light of life
to seep through tiny spaces...

your destiny awaits.

Sucking in the draught of new air which burns the lungs
forcing it to thrust out into the open life, yet it doesn't feel
like freedom...

Lungs once covered with the sticky mucus of a womb and
comforting love...

are now wrapped in the confusion of being abruptly
snatched from a place where all was safe.

Pushed out, but ready.

Snap!

Untethered.
Untethered from the safety of the umbilical cord - pushed
out into a space already cold - the world.

Pausing painfully, birthed into life,
barely here, but stilled,

unable to breathe.

I know this Tongue Gives Life

So I speak in whispers, shouting loudly,

birthing sons and daughters from cracks in concrete

into existence where no one believes and no one cares, or so

it seems.

No one believed life existed.

They left tattered and torn souls to rot to hell

believing only that life was gone and hope had stepped off long ago sending lifeless, hopeless remnants of souls out into the darkness with no expectations and perfectly virgin. Perfectly virgin, knowing only one chip of the underworld and armed with no ammunition for this life's world.

With coal in place of eyes which were long overlooked by fat creatures, dressed in red, sliding down non-existent chimneys. The red matching their eyes and the many blood drops of thoughts as they lay awake believing not in fairy tales but in their own kaleidoscope-colored existence. An existence seemingly broken before the gunshot of the beginning of the race...

The gunshot they mistook as life's background noise on everyday repeat performance of:

Brothers, mothers, sisters, lovers …

snuffed into already-martyred candle shrines, lighting every corner from where they be from...

"Here's your book bag, son…"

It hung loosely from his already-slumped, ten-year old shoulders. His back slightly bent forward from the weight he carries inside, his teeth unbrushed, for yet another day sparkling with gold remnants of toaster strudels from last week and oodles of noodles nestled, nestled in cracks only showing signs of existence from a vaporized gas of sour breath,

he breathed...

He picked up his basketball, placed his mixed-matched socks on his unwashed feet,

one sock his and the other one pink, belonging to his sister on his father's side.

The ash from the stomped out grassless playgrounds crowned and crowded in flattened beads of rings stretched up and around his ankles, he had no Vaseline to set them both free so they stayed, permanently, and became a part of him supporting his stance...

His thin, ash-worn legs,

Feet unwashed...

his head anointed with caps of unknown fury. A crown of thorns, his crucifix of onyx chiseled long ago from some ancestor of the 60's who dared to walk the freedom walk into the light, only to have his legacy of futures trampled and burned to the ground alongside of the once-defeated, upside-down, white crosses which littered hearts and lawns and even dangled fruit, forbidden…

Strange…

Strange fruit, the masterwork of white hoods with holes,

holes held down by brothers tripping over not sagging nor relaxed jeans but bitter genes, DNA…

fighting not to be pushed into forgotten-ness because they had to … they had to exist.

While it was the plan all along, to aim and fire at Kings and symbols of X's and unknown Freedom Riders and Abolitionists fighting chains which would seal and lock them into unmentioned eternities. The murdered and leave them not to be remembered, nor martyred, nor revered.

Brothers and fathers and sons

laying in streets for hours and hours and hours with chalked lines…

not in Selma,

no, not in Mississippi,

NO!

These candlelight rituals be RIGHT HERE!

RIGHT HERE in places where chalk lines are never washed away by rain,

….they are permanent…

"It's time for school boy…"

He, the silhouette of the man that could be the future though unlikely as futures don't exist past twenty-five here…

Opened the refrigerator out of routine.
It was empty …

His stomach ached, growling; he'd eat the free breakfast at school today.

Angry already as tightness gripped his ribs, wondering if his Eve existed…

(part played by mama for now).

For now, she was the Eve of his rib, and ironically would be there on the eve of his epitaph, watering his rose, grown from the ash of the chalk on the crack of any playground 'round here.

His role be ADAM, the original man.

Not being the first man, but being the dream of the FUTURE first man from where he be from…

She was/is a baby mama who sends postcards of Happy Father's Day to herself once a year forgetting often how to unchain her breast to feed even her own child.

"Happy Father's Day Eve"…

SHE follows breadcrumbs of hope herself. Finding only little make-believe gingerbread houses with *for real* ovens open and ready to roast them both!

Ovens ready to roast them whole,
whole the excrements from her own womb.

Children with legacies.

No kiss goodbye.
No nighttime lullabies.

Kool-aid coloring and beans with fried bologna still staining her curved-down lips, should never-EVER to be mistaken for a smile.

No smile either exists for him, either!

He takes his key and locks the door,
pure irony!

LOCK IT IN! LOCK IT IN! LOCK IT IN!

Your fears, silent tears, dreams, shameless shames, her heartbeat, yours too!

LOCK IT IN!

Unwrapping the morning breakfast on his desk a single, silent, but *brave* tear escapes and falls.

It escaped the unexplained rage from within.

"I DON'T LIKE THIS FOOD!"

Soft tongue whispers,

"Take your seat, turn to page 65.

Don't get started today;
it's too early for that, anyway".

With a whisper that shouts loudly,

"I KNOW YOU HEAR ME, UNLOCK IT;
HERE'S THE KEY! EDUCATION WILL SET YOU FREE!"

I teach…

I know this tongue gives life, so I speak in whispers, shouting loudly, birthing sons and daughters from cracks in concrete into existence when no one believes and no one cares…

or, so it seems...

The Block

I'm driving down our street, bowing my head at the threads of balloon candle shrines along the way, counting them. Each signifying the taking of souls from days and nights of existing here... the legacy is clear.

A guy steps out from his stroll with a pole holding a sign, deep in his grind, it read,

"I'M SELLING GOOD KARMA".

I shrugged and dropped a coin hoping to buy some for me and him (mostly me), wondering always, "How could this be?"

I left a place where a lady hung low, kissing the ground while her kids hung around...

what dope of trade would have her degrade
herself?

Lifeless,
self-less yet selfish, kids left for doom ...

shouting out like sonic booms, "*Damn girl! That ain't ya hair! And he ain't ya daddy, and neva was*"!

Flinging back strays of plats loosening at the scalp, looking like mops of yarn matted and patted. Money's short.

Money's short, but he be about that life...

Wading on corners night after night, slinging and stashing...

Crumpled tissues line his pockets,
life's years line his cheeks and tears could always find their tracks and the tissues could find the place to wipe them away.

Wipe them away, as if each wipe were the years and oh, not to mention the tears wasted, because they couldn't help him face it...

"Hey, you got a quarter?"

That phrase on constant rewind...

"Here's to life" , his t-shirt read...

Parables, when life ain't really life, but it mirrors its dark twin ... (but why death gotta be dark?),

Maybe it's light, maybe it could make this imitation of life ... right.

Red, white and blue stripes, and a single star: selling futures for Dreamers in the form of green, furry whispers, the skin of kiwi, and the sweet soul of mango!

"Yo mommi, you want to buy? Icee! Coconut plantain!"

That face of brown gold, forced a loathed smile and a gasped sigh when I denied to buy. The muffled voice whispered, "negro!"

"NEGRO! Man, please!"

Ageless creases of lost smiles right-side up frowns grace the medleys of blended-yet-living-apart-yearning souls, drifting like castaways. All brought *here* or dropped *there,*
all serving the purposes of Willie Lynch knots and still, no pot of gold or 40 acres neither…

We are the mules!

"HEY! you wanna buy this paper or
not?" Snapped back by local realities…

*"Okay, just give me 20 for this EBT, stash…
you get 50…I need the cash."*

I turned the corner now my smile is upside down and my whisper was that other 'n' word as I watched *her* child stand by *her* side like an open wound. She hung low, real low,

dipping to a slow-motioned song in her head…the walking dead…

never falling, indicating she had more drop to go. She had slipped long ago from her golden throne but her princess, with a single snotty tear stain line gracing her face, guarded her mother's side waiting for a dime from a kind stranger walking by...

                ME,

but while examining the broken gems fallen from the crown peaks, I recognized them as family jewels...

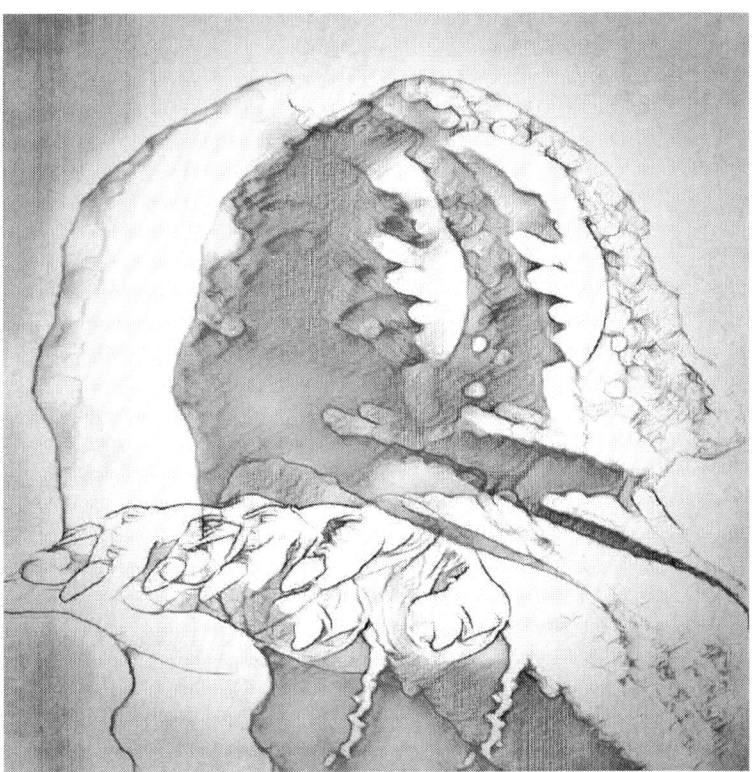

I took one step, dropped a 50 in the vein-splintered hand and walked away slowly, tearfully, clasping the princess's hand in mine, heading home…to my home, on the block…

A single whisper in a stare between us…

Auntie to princess: *"I got you now…hold on."*

She was the daughter of Lot..
and before backward glances turned them all to stone and crumbled them to dust in lives passed away…

she turned back to look,

but only once before remembering she was to be reborn like a Phoenix from this nightmare…

All the while she was just a kid from the block….

A piece of coal saved in the ashes of a burnt-out phoenix's thrust,

My sister's child…

Seconds Clean

They be clapping…

Saying and celebrating your years clean…

"Yay, you did it!"

I sit, silent, with applause inside my eyes…

Clap…clap…clap…

Each clap like thunder, rippling,
with my heartbeat; here's to you…

You with your underlying abuse. Freedom...

Here's to me...
Because I'm still walking around with this monkey on MY back.

Yet YOU, YOU be free…

I'm still caught in chains of burnt out pain.

Mom,

I haven't been freed...I'm still tied to leaning poles, holding the geometry of life by the angled-side.

90 degrees of childhood lost!
360 degrees of madness!

I hold on to the angles of spent realities,

Trying to keep them from falling,
and catching my tears as they slide down your tilted spine,
dipping but not hitting earth...

But I'm strong; I have the strength

> of a child's essence,
> of burnt in fortitude,
> of being silenced,
> of tears, of rage

that run inside of fear,
of no way of showing love
without showing hate,

> of self,
> of fear,
> of you returning,

To HER, the monster of my youth.
She still hides under beds, in closets,
in the threads of my worn out knees.

My chest heaves of crying that never stops.

When I'm allowed to breathe, I choke…
I choke up you.

I fear seeing leaning poles because they remind me - each and every one of them - of you.

Endless corners with cans, EBT cards, newspapers, kids clothes...

        mine…

You selling them for crack, not food.

Mom, I'm zero minutes,
zero days,
zero months,
zero years…

free.

No, no one freed me…
I sit in silence while you are praised;
weak ass'd excuses for my hell.

I stood silent through it all.

Where is my applause?

My award for a super f'd up life
which taught me 2 things:

>how not to die,
>and how to *fight*.

When hands lift, and before they meet again, vibrating with sound which creep into my coal mine of a heart… I sit silent.

You glance at my silence holding in fear,: for it holds secrets. It's clap is like thunder.

Holding the strength to crack and break through
silence. So I see how you might be scared,
Scared for me to speak.

We are grateful we made it; made it past late evenings of street walks, 2 a.m. freedom calls,

missed class trips, deep nods thru parent meetings,

>*Yours…*

Those gold stockings with holes you wore to pick me up from school…

      well at least you came…

And that Afro-matted wig you wore to my graduation, smelling like a spilled drink.

The fights I'd get into after kids snickered about you…

The hunger
for food and
for life.

The pain of being a child from the temporarily-motherless clan.

Your skeleton frame, your toothless grin,
my never-new clothes, my unkempt 6 year old self...

Your screams through playground fences at my lunchtime recess. Me pretending not to know you.
My missed school days, my smells, yours too.
My reflection in mirrors, hoping
not to become you.

My screams the day they took me from school in that black car, from you…

black clouds of thunder, scared,
left lonely last night and the other night and the other,

when you didn't come home for me.

8 years of foster care,
12 years of blank black stares,
20 years clean,
20 nights of tears and heart screams,
my 20 years of living *me-without-you.*

I hear the claps and congrats and I smother the rage within,
warming the coal, begging
to erupt and form MY diamond!

It's like the irony of saying happy birthday to the child when the mom bore the pain,

except mine is in reverse…

They be clapping, I be sitting
silent, waiting…for the encore…

waiting,

for MY applause.

Angel Down

I am lost somewhere between sunrise and sunset, but not the final one.

Tear struck, crumbled pieces of love and heart, not sure which is which as I turn from them, blowing and scattering…

the mere departure of the pieces of lost heart is too much to bear.

Wishing every tear away, saddened I hadn't taken the time to make you right…as if I had the power anyway.

Trying my hardest to hold back and refrain from crying, no screaming out in pain, muffled by visions…so I slowly closed my eyes and held my ears too, not to hear the sounds that also held the "on" switch for memories…

My soul escaped my body and found you in the moment just before IT happened…

oh the rapture…

Fear gripped, adrenaline pumped; he raised the gun, eyes exploded. Many thoughts of love and life I'd not see, time stood still, he pulled the trigger...

Fear was my companion...

Slow motion movies of you picking me up, throwing me high into the air...symbolic of how you dreamt I'd soar through life..

Tears burned, chest opened, body pained
...burned...pain...light...fire...more light...

and then the wind kissed my breath and claimed it back as its own...

In not knowing where to run and who could run in slow motion anyway...I saw them running by...and I felt without feeling that I should hate...all were crying...

fueled with anger, not fear, filled with a longing for me...but I am right here..

I am an angel, an angel downed...
graceful, loving you always, you don't have to say goodbye, I'm right here....

Mamas don't be angry, for they know not what they do...
Write the words of memories of my smile on their hearts; it will lift your heart and caress your mind...I'm right there, reach out...feel me...the chalk line on the ground will soon fade...

And even though my obituary will be empty as I have not lived long enough for an entry, a thought, a memory, a gift, a longing....let your tears keep the ink of an unwritten soul's words...and though those words hold infinity, life is finite, help them, help them break the cycle..

Mamas, don't be mad, mamas don't be sad…the verses are written and the ink is dry…in your moments of sanctuary, cry, but not for me; change those that live. Oh Mama, give!

Give! Give them what you tried to give me; teach them, grasp your heart to their mind and don't let them go…only then can I, your angel, be free. I am an angel, an angel downed…graceful, loving you always. You don't have to say goodbye. I am right here.

They Speak to My Soul

They speak to my soul with haikus, similes, and the laughter of sonnets. Some blue, some are tragedies, some are wild, free verses of soliloquies and metaphoric wonder...

Their lives, in the form of teardrop-crystals with pointy edges, pierce my soul daily...

When I close my eyes I see the sons of the sun's rays of tomorrow, and tomorrow *IS* brilliant..

When I hug my shoulders I feel feelings of lifting chains and freedom from worries and lives loved unconditionally...they love me.

Trust...trusts flows in free stanzas like limited sonnets of truths and fairytales of lives given, and some taken, and some, yes, some become life givers way too soon. Caught in cycles of endless infinities of hopelessness but yet they, and their hearts, remain hopeful.

And, if - just if -they don't know doom, they can live freely, unchained because with puberty comes knowledge of nakedness and a forced existence of acceptance,

acceptance that lives don't live in poems,
they live in the *forreal-forreal*....unless...

unless children become poets, then they too can write their own lives in stanzas of freedom and creative free-verse, so breathe...breathe haikus and diminished, hexagonal beats that rise and fall with your own heart; it will save your life...

Children...grow up,
                      and be poets.

Open Windows

First floor classrooms with open windows allow breezes, smells, wanderings of neighborhood laughter, tears, joys and years…

But, yesterday was the mark of a new day.

In yesterday, I saw the beginnings of today…
Hot springs of breezes, swirling, made for windows to be opened high.

Words, shouts, and non-whispers of
passersby, just outside my classroom…

With the breezes THEY floated in.
Unwanted sounds, drifting up and around, corrupting…
sounds like…

"Hey how much? What can a 20 buy?"

"Listen poppi, open you fly!"

"I got it in"
"Pay me, don't you owe me 10?…"

Open Windows...Open Ears...

"Ray, pay attention!
Close that window, Jen!"

Me watching candid faces and young eyes which pierce hearts,

as my thighs and knees tremble because
I have to keep my hand steady,
and my thoughts and tongue completely ready.
I teach...

Math lessons were more like,

"How much can I make a night dancing poles, Miss? That seems right; Imma ask my auntie she does it nights..."

Showing me rolls of money and minks she hadn't stole...

"I don't need math, I'm gonna follow her path."
She getting paid, and her , well she just slays..."

History began with granny, mommy, auntie and dem,
never ever mentioning the men...makes you wanna ask... is this something from the past?

Like men been sold off the plantation, separated, gone off leaving behind their creation? Black people wake up, this is our nation!

...Technology: what's the fee?

Scrolling countless pages, sudden
stop, Untargeted pops....
Shots fired in the night after a fight
over there in the park, a picture on the web is the mark.

Mama screams;
she gave up the dream and memories,

memories of me, of a boy once cheerful
with joy, who happened to see his dad on the internet for free...

"Miss, my dad's on the computer; please come see.."

Him: *Happy joy!*
Me: annoyed, the caption read:

"Williams captured, 4 dead... 3 wounded....wife bled...out"

Boy taken into custody...
Pure sweet rhapsody, the innocent...irony,

Years would pass, as do the lessons of life,

page after page, then I see you...

"18 year-old burns to death"

Keeping warm with heaters,
uncontrolled fire feeder, baby breeders,
babies burned, mama earned...

Mama earned her living at night
riding poles, dancing stripping clothes, sliding and sniffing,

baby holds her hand out for quarters
to buy... ice...

"Ice, it's cold right?"

But not as cold as days and endless nights
waiting for someone to come. Your heart
begins to run,
and you scream the American Dream, then swallow.

*"Somebody lied! I was told I could be
anything I wanted to be...
Teacher, I don't need math; I make more selling my a**"*

Well how you gonna count your cash? Or know when someone's beat you for your stash?

Years go by, newspapers don't lie;
pages, pages, pages, fly by…

Stop! Count them…
1, 2, 3, 4…

"Please please please no more!
Not Ray Ray too! His mental capacity ruled…"

1 - murder

2 - drugs

3 - gang signs

4 - arson

HE burned souls….

his mama's and mine
Soul screams….he could have been fine…

He could have been,
he could have been,
he could have been...

ANYTHING!

Shots were fired, kids never scurry, some even nodded

"Miss, stop crying, Yea, I know them
That was Ray Ray and dem. Please
stop crying...
Don't cry for me,
I'ma be just fine..

just fine…
I got other friends…

Today is the mark of a new day
I see beginnings …

Hot springs of breezes and burning heat can make us sweat alright...

But today, I'm gonna keep them damn windows closed tight.

I Just Called to Say I Love You...

HE,
pulls himself close to his desk
pen in hand.

Nevermind the glazed-over eyed look of nothingness on his face.

ME,
wondering if he is in fact in the right place.
There is silence between us...

WE
like to play music during our class work space.

THEY
write as I watch.
they talk,
I listen...

Then, *IT* energized his soul and the air, like magic often does.
Yes! my main man Stevie Wonder...on full blast;

"I just called to say I love you

I just called to say how much I care,
I just called to say I love you,
And I mean it from the bottom of my heart"

And then, from the deepest forest of the autism spectrum -

HE breathed.

With a refreshed inhale, HE exhaled....
slowly, but evenly.

And with the exhale came a furthered concerto with his voice of:

"No summer's high,
no warm July,
no harvest moon to light one tender August night,
no autumn breeze,
no falling leaves,
not even time for birds to fly to southern skies....".

Eyes wide...mine...
He ...*WAS* ...Stevie!
No, I mean,
Stevie ...*WAS*...him!

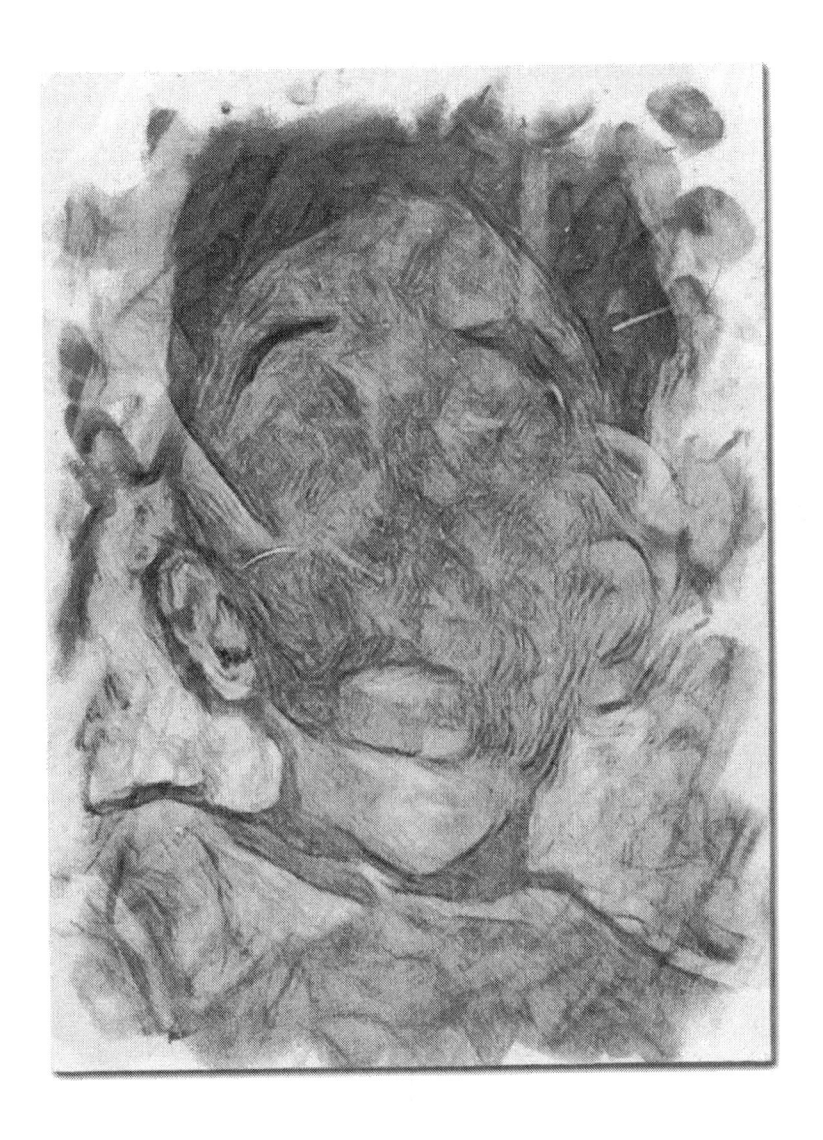

The melodious gasp which waved over his tongue, teeth and lips gushing freely from the core of that which used to be silent now sounded like, like...like a front seat symphony of the king himself!

But it was this BOY,
HIM….

Had our educational system,
The Svengali of urban truths
Created *this*?

This Rain Man?

Had they, life and the lunacy of the school systems seduced him?

Dominated his spirit,
and exploited his 'non worthy' existence?
I mean …

HE SPOKE No words in 80 days of...
120 minutes of math,
120 minutes of Language Arts,
and where fast paced spits of science,
were met with more OF HIS silence!

The Arts and his love for music and open space and gifts of talent were taken and substituted for in-house babysitting blues.

The paint drips on canvas hues in the key of HIS life, gone.

Leaving HIM with his mind filled with luscious melodies.

Rhymes and rhythms,
rhythms and rhymes…
and WHO knew!

"But what it is, though old so new,
to fill your heart like no three words could ever do"

SING STEVIE SING!

FOR HE lived…
and died…
that very same day…back into silence.

Sadly,

test Scores ***don't*** reflect this,
this kind of magic!
So THEY took him.

They took him to that place where all
the broken kids go….

And me, well my heart was left void.
Teachers, teachers, teachers...teach.

I solemnly played his song once or twice since then.
It had changed, it grew to feel sad and needy...no more joy, no wonderment....that was taken along with him.

And now it seems like many moons ago…
5 or 10 years or so…

I'm crossing streets
with thoughts, inside, of what I had to do and who I had to meet.

The crazy man who smelled like hell each and every day,
stopped traffic in his usual way…

always with a smile…FOR ME…

and then, I heard it..

*"I just called to say I love you,
I just called to say how much I care"*

It was magic!

*"I just called to say I love you,
and I mean it from the bottom of my heart…"*

Muffled between the coins in his dirty baseball cap

He sang,

that song,

those words……

"I know you…"

He whispered…

*"I just called to say I love you
And I mean it from the bottom of my heart….."*

Where *do* Broken Children go?

Broken Child

The broken child cries silent tears while well-aware of his own hurts and fears,

      he cries loudly but silently.

The broken child has piercing eyes where sunshine sparkles once did reside,

he has black tunnels void of hope where shadows are found but no person.

The broken child spews the loudest cry for help as he covers swollen welts,

      he is beaten into non-existence.

If broken wombs shelter the tomorrows, then reflections will recognize future horrors. The shelter is weak so the foundation is sure to fold.

And if broken worlds spew forth broken souls, the children's spirits will enter holes. They can't seem to break free. They are prisoners - beaten, abused, as angry broken people amuse themselves and

he is prostituted to the world without shame.

Broken child,

why do they wonder why you can't succeed?

Are you trying as you bleed?

He bleeds broken blood, non-transparent.

He lives in a world where broken smiles are prominent frowns and there's no justice…

or so it seems this child loses …

Broken child,
it's funny but somehow strange,
that your dreams will not be broken, only deranged…

For broken children have no other dreams,
they just repeat the inevitable cycle.

Our Streets

Our streets have tattoo markings penned in blood - burnt dry by the sunless light of gunfire, SON-LESS !

Night after night, muzzled only by the cries of screeching tires, firing away. Birds sing of gunfire blasts, crows sound like fireworks, eating the flesh left behind, basking under street lights which used to have voices, voices which called children home at dusk…and they still do…children answer from other lifetimes.

Hearts still beat through tears and fears of mothers as they lift voices in high pitches matching the cords of others. Night comes quietly lifted only by sirens and red flashing lights to signal those left behind through the dusk. Tomorrow is coming, and at dusk, yet another mother will call out "BRING MY CHILD BACK TO ME", and wait with perseverance for dusk to answer.

Dear Broken Girl

Dear Broken Girl,

It's a world that has never been true so why do *you* expect it to break it's character and be true, to you?

If you left it (your heart I mean), it would break you down.

And if you offer it (your spirit) the world will wipe it, and you, away….

it's not safe to play…

to play with fire, no matter what the desire. You sit idle, still wishing you could be noticed.

> He won't.
> She can't;
> you don't exist.

You fade some, because transparency is easier than reality at times…

Children of the bed,

you know...bastards, those of the unwed...

the shafted lives, the penalty of the parents' immature taste of the forbidden...

Never ever out-live it,

and *IT* can't be overwritten...

They don't carry the last name of the father, only the blood with no title....

Dear broken girl,
don't take it personally...

He moves on, She moves on...but you, not you, you get left, not in body, but in spirit...

Who do *you* belong to?

You feel caught and somehow you are never the right fit... So, you lie.

You lie and say "he is dead" when they ask, but he isn't;

but he may as well be...he's *nothing* to you.

Dear Broken Girl,

he didn't leave you to abuse, he left you so he could break loose...it's not about you....

Stand frozen, don't move,

maybe they won't notice… Fatherless,

loveless, nobody notices…

When his eyes began to look at you…like you were his….

when his hands began to touch you…wishing you were his…

skin crawls, hate crawls…

this is not the love you're looking for.

And she pretends…

She pretends not to know, not to hear.

She pretends not to,

but she does not ever face that she had to love you for

two, two people…

This is the end of an affair of the bed…

a child,

a mother

and a man…

Broken promises, broken dreams,

Broken family because none ever existed,

Broken him leaving a child to the wilds,

Broken her with long lasting broken smiles…

The virgin no longer exists, petals gone, blown from her midst...settling like a purple badge traded for a passing kiss.

Broken eyes spew broken tears down broken cheeks and flow nowhere.

Nowhere is where your broken spirit hides,
holding a broken key to a broken heart...

but that broken key magically still fits and opens the channel to broken knocks....

knocks which leave you flat ... *Broke-in*.

Dear Broken Girl,
what's within can never be spoiled...

he can't love you,
she won't love you

and they don't know...he wants to...
but that's not love,
be strong...it's all wrong.

What does it leave you?

You love hard and you hurt deep.
You find it hard to sleep,
sleep...without clothes.

Without clothes you feel unprotected and exposed, not safe.

When they love and leave...they have crushed yet another inch of your guarded place, your heart...

No soft kisses, brings back the memories. So you don't kiss....
ever.

No connections, you're too afraid.
You *can't*, so he can't,
but you expect him to.

Dear Broken Girl,
you play with broken toys in a broken world and expect nothing less than perfection.

He came back and looked into your eyes...
deep into that place and you? Silly you,
silly in love with being loved and tired of searching for it, so you let him in.

You forgot,

nobody wants a broken toy....

even if they were the one who broke It.

Dear Broken Girl,

living in a broken world...don't pass it on...leave it.

Broken things become blessed things because they learn from experience how to fight harder and fighting harder isn't always a physical thing

You try to remember this, but maybe your connection is static....maybe,

it's broken as well.

I Promised Her

I promised her I would…
expel the myths of why she would have to hide the traces of the scared tat that read, *"Me too"*.

Carved long before it was sexy to the world and considered a right to bear the need to run from the despair of the label,

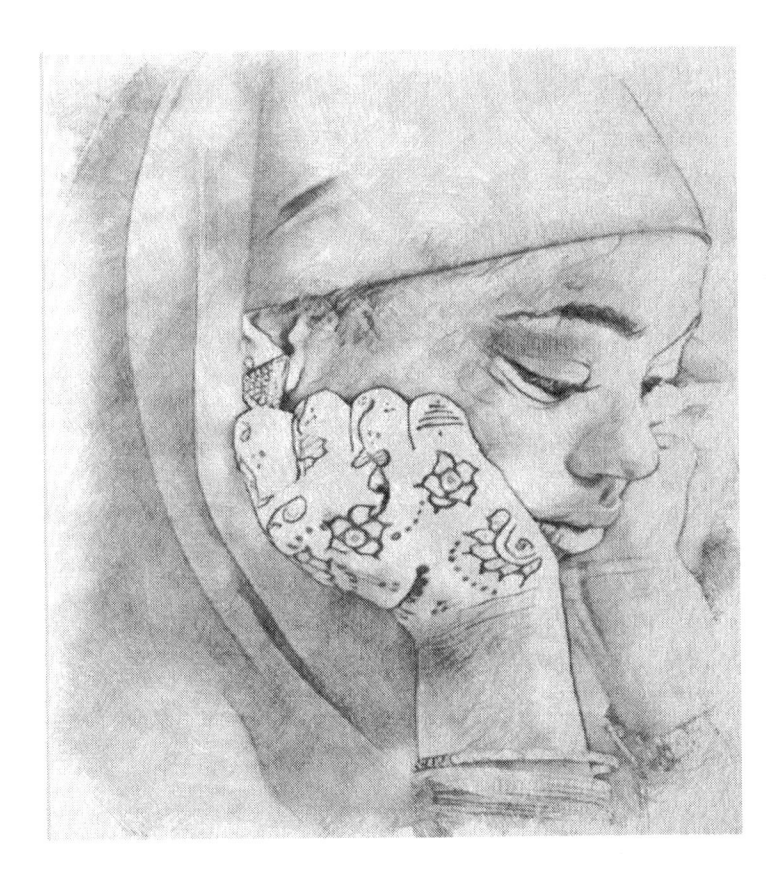

Much harder than the life that brought it forth, *me too*. I promised her the truth. Rough hands of abuse as she shed tears in mirrors long ago, dropped and broken,

plaguing life with 7 more…

7 years of bad luck, no relief. Then death brought her belief,

and I stood on the edge of his grave
hoping my lines of cracked, broken tears shed long ago could fade and save her lifeless soul.

Never having lived, never having been loved,
restrained, not knowing how to give.

I promised her I'd speak,
I'd give up being meek,
I'd fight, I'd yell…I'd scream her misery to hell.

What kind of people take the souls of children and hand them shame instead?

What kind of people erase happiness and place fear in their heads?
What kind of mothers turn their heads

when their own come home broken and
bled, but say nothing?

She whispers... *me too.*

Begging others to hear it through running tears, dropping slurs…"what's wrong?"

She struggled to stand tall, trying to scream,
me too,

but dust-filled whispers came out instead…
Filling urns with souls just like hers, those
who never really earned their fate,

I promised her …

So, I took up the lit-torch, feeling nothing…

Too gated, too chained, too guarded, too angry, too, too much like her…

I wiped his filth from me, wrapped a
towel round my world, Stepped
forward, ripped open my chest,

finally,

to allow myself to rest…

Exposing my tattoo that read…..

"ME TOO!"

She…was….me…

I didn't whisper,

I yelled…

"ME TOO!"

I promised her…

She is Beautiful...

I can see her soul…

Fighting the battle of a queen when the world tells her to bow down.

I looked at her like I needed someone to look at me,

"you're beautiful".

She looked back at me
and I think for the very first time
really looked at me…

HER *reflection.*

Me, tracing the lines in her forehead,
they told it all…

Yet, there was no belief in her stare.

Maybe there was a time,

a time before when her reflection looked more like beauty and less like pain.

Maybe it faded and was
long lost to unfulfilled dreams,
covered by harsh realities.
So her heart forgot what her soul could not.

Ya Malikah, you're beautiful....

The blank, black eyes again…

They pierced mine,
reminding me of the *Houris*
-the faithful feminine beauties found only in *Jannah,*
and places where angels and good beautiful souls sit in rank
below only God.

SHE belonged there…

I ask, have you really forgotten?
I mean, doesn't the "*YOU*" in you know you?

Here, take *it*...
the dragonflies brought *it* back,
your *soul* to your mind,
your *mind* to your heart refined,
your *heart* to your body these are the signs.
WHO ARE YOU?

Do you miss her?

Do you miss the *you* before you had heartbreak or before you met betrayal?

The you before the truth of life had you witness and forced you to embrace?

Do you miss the YOU of you?

The YOU before the years reproduced themselves ....over and over and over...
 until the seams of your soul seemed lost.

Ya Malikah, you're beautiful....

Do you miss the you that once trusted?
The you that once believed in happy endings and forever.
The you that wasn't afraid to give it all and believed in honesty.

The you that was willing to wrap arms around the present knowing there was a future.
The you without the guarded heart.

Ya Malikah, you're beautiful....

Here, hold it,
I passed her my reflection…

And her eyes surrendered to sight.

Tears creased her chin and dropped memories to her heart..

And finally, she could honestly see and believe,

SHE WAS BEAUTIFUL...

His Shoes

Ain't much to really talk about...
They were shoes, walking beats every day.

I didn't try to understand why a boy,
soon to be a man,
needed so many pairs.

But there was something about those shoes.

Keeping secrets,
standing quietly on their own, as if they were waiting for him.

OH SHOES…
how many places had you accompanied him to?

YOU seem to hold tears too.

Dust shifted from the toe shafts as they were lifted from their resting place on the ground,

showing a grace of sadness as only old shoes do.
A single, strong arm

just simply couldn't fling them up on the power line.
In front of HIS house...the martyr's shrine.

Hanging from laces in the sky, like so many before him, gone on to die...

Dust shifted back into its place, leaving only footprint outlines like chalk on concrete grounds...the dirt from the playground below clung tightly to the soles;

isn't it funny how even his shoes had a soul?

Laces fringed, life lines ripped from this realm, tongues now silent....

The neighborhood creeps, keeping secrets,
shoes left without an owner...a soul escaped.

Threads stretched, color once-vibrant, now fading from the sun's attention with each life second ticking by and each tick suffocates with unmasked rain tears which trickle down to the toe, to the ground, tracing the sole as it departs.

If only they could talk....

where did you go with him? And why did he leave you behind?

Ain't much to really talk about...

They were only shoes...his shoes,
I flung them up high on the power wire myself...hoping to give them a safe place...

eternal life.

Polyptotons

Power tends to corrupt, and absolute power corrupts absolutely.

There is no end of it, the voiceless wailing.

No end to the withering of withered flowers,
to the shackled freedom that is not free and not liberating,

To the drift of the sea and the drifting wreckage of the African Diaspora…

souls dispersed but never forgetting
(you can't untie a knot)…bound to souls whispering "bring our children back; they will never be forgotten."

Oh, Children of the Diaspora…

Let's stand where our shoulders meet with our whole selves feet to feet.

It doesn't matter what shore we met
as we departed on their wretched fleet.

Let our human souls make sound and speak,
listen daily to the rhythm of the beat.

The cancered bone's prayer of Death is to God only.

Prayers for the one emancipated through a fake emancipation, celebrating Juneteenth as if that freed them souls!

And let's not talk about the minds…

oh, don't forget the unforgettable…

    lest We forget,
        lest We forget,
            don't forget…

Remembering is the opener of the secrets to get off the merry-go-round of repeat…

and who called it *merry* anyway?

No, there is no end to the violence of the violent, nor the prayer of the prayerful, nor the tears of the tearful;

Every day in the hood of the neighborhood where moms outlive their life-less youth...

And where teachers teach to the muted hearts of the heartful, and heart-less too..

All numb to life yet youthful enough to live...

(even if it's short).

No solemn words for the eulogy...ALL youth go to heaven anyway...don't they?

In neighborhoods where neighbors live life into lifeless journeys which are encircled with circles of cycles of generation after generation producing fresh springs of offspring yet offering them up for sacrifice to the lords and landlords, I mean to the warlords of the streets they be fighting for...

The streets that ain't even theirs...

And nobody questions why the warriors fight wars for street territories and not hills of mansions where the gold of the gold mines of their lost forefathers still remain without the traces of the minds mines they stole it from when they robbed the tombs of our fathers', fathers', fathers...

The pristine gardens of Eden,
Adam's first footsteps…

Ivory husks,
a human cargo…
blood diamonds…

papyrus of papers of legitimacy, which ripped their births
from rippled nations...

And I'm still laughing out loud at the origin of *that* word,
Where now they have corrupted the sound and the meaning:

> *Niger,*
> *Nye-ger,*
> *Nee-ger,*

But I remember the river Niger...
And I remember that other 'N' word
and it ain't NEVER pronounced in French!

Besides guys from the hood
still trying to convince the world of *ebonics* for the ebony
hue...
Heck I need a translation!

Some are too young to know, or too old to care...
And they massacred more than our heroes long ago...

The massacred left only
a legacy of cycles of the cycle of dead ends...

But in their neighborhoods there are no dead places…

They live life on cul-de-sacs…

Their circles re-cycle generations of what never belonged to them anyway…

Take back your gold,
Constant reminders to the mind…
YOU can remember your holocaust as to not live life reliving your own massacre on purpose.

Polyptotons suggest change.

Different forms of a repeated word can also suggest something more subtle than contrast;

It can suggest change from one state to another
Just as the repeated word changes from one form to another,

Polyptotons
mimic life.

Breathing...

Everything wind kissed
softens the soul

***

Having patience is a gift;
you don't know the blessing
until you are tested

***

If you have the ability to love,
love freely,
but love yourself first.

***

There's nothing lonelier
than truly being alone with a soul,
that is broken and barren.
Love something with your soul;
dream something with your
heart, or, at least, try to…

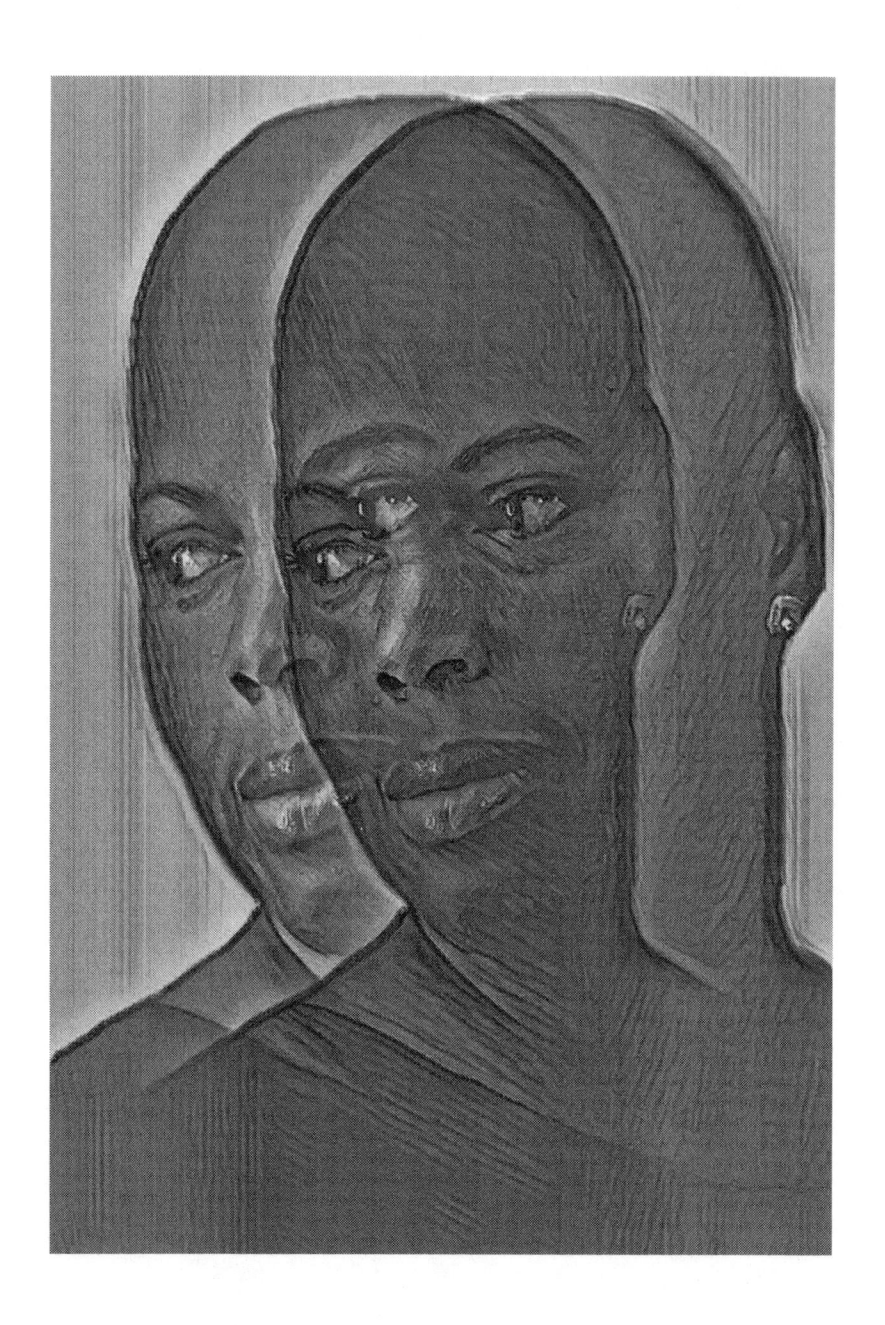

***

Tears heal,

tears wash,

tears hold memories,

drop after drop…

***

It is only truth

which keeps your beauty pure;

natural,

untouchable,

but lasting.

***

Souls cry softly.

Observe the eyes,

these cannot lie;

your eyes were brilliant.

***

Loud whispers,

no one hears

***

There's no broken heart,
which truly mends
completely.

***

"I'm sorry"
never means
it's okay
to lay down
your armor.

***

You're in there somewhere,
waiting for rebirth.
Close your eyes,
call them back.
The wind spent
moments of self
put the pieces into place
Start with the eyes.
They are safe

***

Her voice so raspy
from cigarettes.
Yet in my memory
it warms my thoughts
like a soft berceuse -
a soft, melodic lullaby.
Losing a precious soul is never easy
when you are trying to hold onto
the sanity of your own mind.

***

Beautiful Naturally

All the things I thought to be hard,
you made easy.

When I felt I needed to hold your hand and nurture you, you struck a pose poised with your electric smile, and stood on top of the highest throne, next to your crown and hugged humanity.

When I looked at the sun in its early rising and thought of its beauty, you smiled and the sun lost its place.

You illuminated the moon and the stars caught fire from your essence; your eclipse displaced depressed scents of sad souls and delivered them to happiness.

Your strengths, your dignity neatly placed by Allah, bleed out to others just by passing into, and out of, your presence.

A synonym for you is Beauty…your middle name is Grace…
Your heart melts kindness…You are beautiful.
Smile, the world needs your blessing….

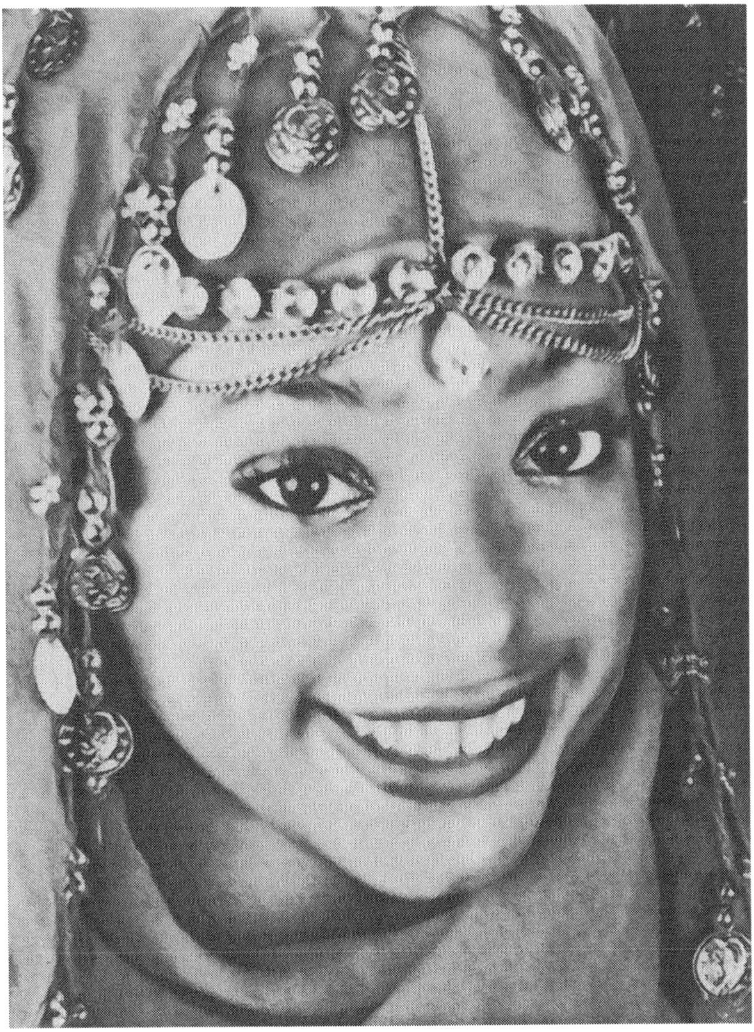

Fires of Memories

One day I couldn't find any paper to write my memories of you, so I wrote them on my heart.

They were written with fires that burnt of inward tears that drizzled down the softened spikes in my throat like crystals in caverns, dripping with fury,

only to drown as there were way too many.
Too many tears wasting into warm acid oceans, burning all they touched,

leaving no space for the final moment, the opening of the flood gates.

When breath, heart beats, twitching eyes,
salt and the angels are present to relieve this realm of souls, carrying the prized essence of life from this space, this world, into twinkled spaces of stars into the forever. Memories stay behind to mourn.

I learned to miss you. I learned to welcome shooting stars - broken off pieces of the fire from the universe. They are allowed to visit us and fill voids of hopelessness and loneliness.

A year makes a big difference, lived without you…

I can honestly say, I hate darkness.
What if stars and the broken pieces of hope filled every space of every night?

Leaving no spot undone, I wouldn't need paper or memories then, I'd see you…darkness would be gone.

Reflect

She searched passionately
through garbage cans along littered,
smelly streets,

holding out crumbled
hands for passersby.

Quarters,

Liquid from used paper cups, bite marks around the softened
rims (like her soul).

Dimes,

cigarette butts, used condoms - hers, his... she tossed them.
Useless life stems. Counting change with dirty fingernails,
showering only when it rains.

I watched, as I often do,

from behind rose colored glasses,
so cliché.

Thinking,

I'M NOT YOU!

Disgust bubbles my intestines.
My mind is not free.
Thoughts flow unconfused, except when it comes to you.

I HATE YOUR EXISTENCE!

We share blood,
bone and marrow...
my blood stains from the rage of pain.
I'm torn and shallow.

You lift your head for me momentarily
as you smell my presence.
I put on my protective shield, it renders me invisible…
my secret power.

I WISH YOU WERE!

Scars of my heart
tell me reality is not far
but I can't hide. It's beginning to fade, back to madness.

You, in a moment of sanity
from the self-imposed land of
insanity, recognize, *YOU SPEAK!*

I do not even see you (illusions from my mind).
There's a lump of pain in human form in front of me
and I dare not acknowledge.

As salaamu alaikum,

...*I DON'T KNOW YOU!*

Eyes peep above shallow, dark rims.
White crusty dry lips.
Chalk-like, stained mucus, crusty on edges,
hold tight to your nostrils.
Rough patched pieces of skin laced together
in thin vertical lines grow into and out of each other holding
 together a resemblance of a face.

Not MINE!

Hallowed eyes…
your eyes were always that puke sort of green.
I remember them,

before the haze.

I stood stupefied in a daze.
"Ameerah do you know her?",

asked the haunted voice of sanity in my soul.
I do not answer.

With an unsteady hand, I put the cracked mirror I'd been holding slowly back in the trash. I was rummaging through; it held too many truths.

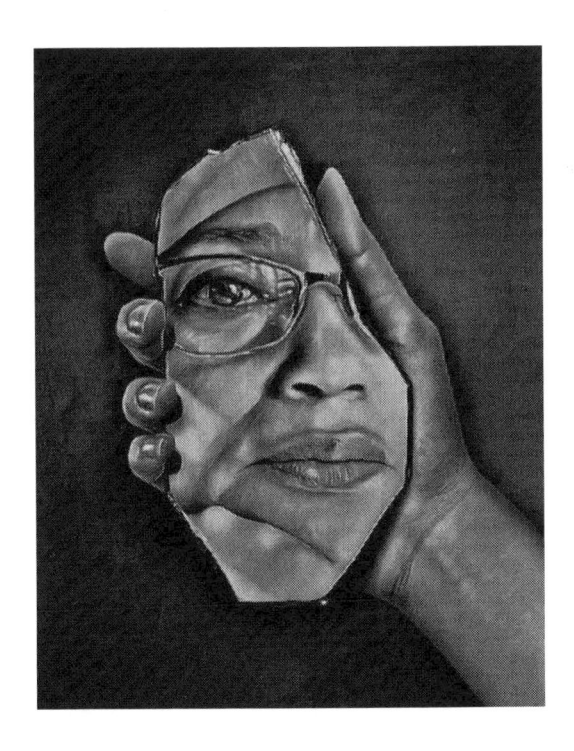

My eyes never leaving the piled treasure of nothingness.
In the cracks of my life, this mirror,
I see distorted reflections.

I pause,
inhale, then
exhale.
I swear this ain't breathing!

Insanity consumed my freedom!
Claiming me back into its hallows.
I retreated with a peaceful ease.
Back into blackness, fades to nowhere.

I feel safer there….I can breathe.

Grateful

She laughed with taunting smiles at how my son was doomed from the beginning.

By knowing me...

She constantly asks me why I am not more like so and so. Or, why I waste my time in corners on corners blowing stacks of smoke into nowhere.

Using smelly blunts dropped and left behind by strangers, I blow endless smoke signals for help in rings that evaporate into nothingness...

My life.

She wonders why I fall into place in a blinded pace when HE calls.

She wonders why I often trip and fall walking hurried steps into nowhere.

She laughs out loud at the worn out clothes of my son.

She wipes the snot from his nose whispering swears in his ears about me.

My son wears shoes too big.
My baby wears pants so high.

I give him knee socks to hide his ankles from the world.

We eat honey buns and water laced orange aid for dinner. We brush our teeth with wash cloths and wipe stains away from our mouths with the back of our hands.

She laughs and shakes her head as my son's pace is slowed by his way too big shoes.

She turns and glares at me and says "your baby can't run he's gonna lose".

I take food from shelters on weekends.
I walk to places where clothes dumpsters run over, finding gems. Some name brands having been passed down from hand to hand now rest gracefully in mine. I gratefully accept.

Maybe they aren't so big, and even if they are, he will not outgrow them soon and we'll be good.

These are just a little too high, but I think we can get by.

When I enter our small apartment over the laundromat with
the bags in the late afternoon,

it smells like heaven.

With scents of Fabric Fresh and Tide,
and Downy, and bleach woofing through broken vents,
passages for good things,
crawling things and warm smells of …

did I mention heaven?

No trouble putting dinner on
and we are happy.

She is nowhere around.
Peace, solace, and love can be found.

And we are grateful
My son, and me.

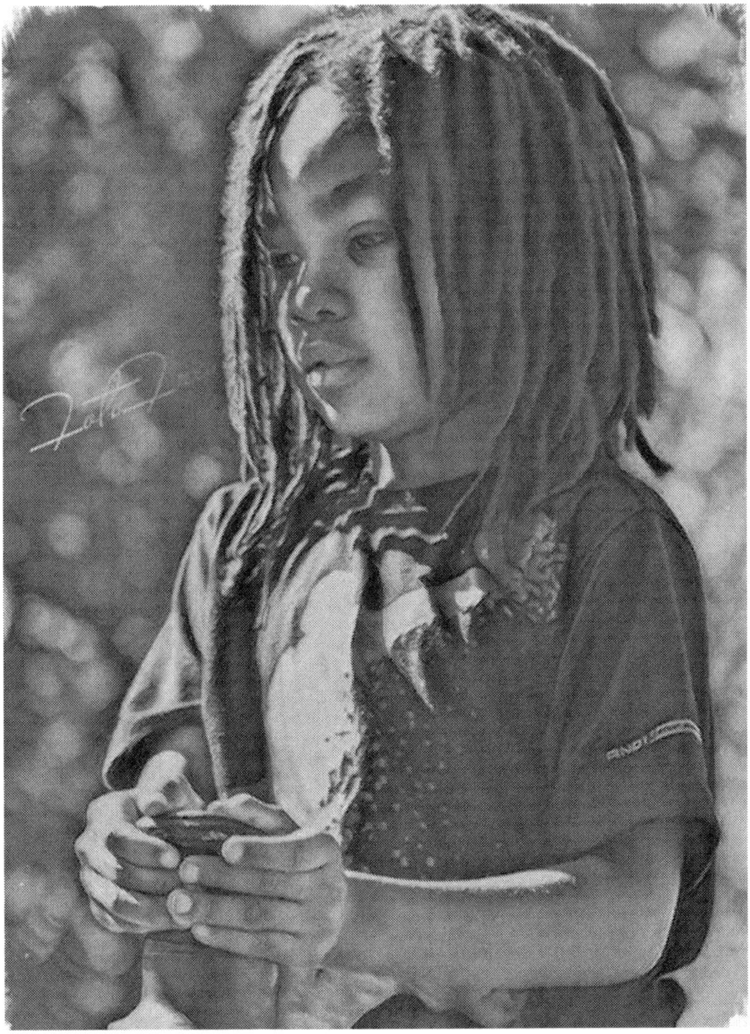

Crevices

Cracks,
Corners without light.

Places where children take form.

Liquid,
plastic,
molds,
warm,
cold formed.

It's been written in prophecies
a long time ago, way before me…
way before we.

It's been dipped in nectar, groupings
of future men and women before
they were children born.

Flanked embryos circling in dried out places awaiting turns to breech birth into life.

Encased in darkened caverns...caves, snuggled in the wombs of our mothers...

Waiting for the revolution

>of birth,
>of knowledge,
>of self,
>of recompense,
>of unsolved mysteries,
>of black and blue,
>of me...of you.

Prophecies of legacies of martyrdom,
OF LIVING FREE.

Living without death's brow
on mother's tongues...telling
of how...

>How they'd grow in spite
>>of destiny.

To BE trees.
To be trees fed
with the world's fruits

avoiding always being victims
and becoming strange fruit.

Breathing oxygen, allowing breaths to finally breathe.

Living love,
redemption,
sing that song.

Live in spite of life,
love in spite of knowing death.

Crevices are places where children take form
and neither death nor destruction is the norm.
Live your rebirth, find your redemption song.

To *form,* to *live, in spite of legacies.*

Breathing and Hoping for Wind

I never removed their clothes,
their toys,
or their smells
from this darkened place we called nothing.
Nothing but - the apartment, not home,
just the apartment.

I thought they would, one day, find me
after a binge

so I never left the apartment...

I held on, even after selling most things.
But, I couldn't sell off the love or their scent.
Even if their love was still able to believe in me,
I was already ripped from within. I was a broken recluse from life.

No mending me...

I'd sell them again
if only I could trade off the broken
loneliness and be able to forget...

Their smell, it's still here.

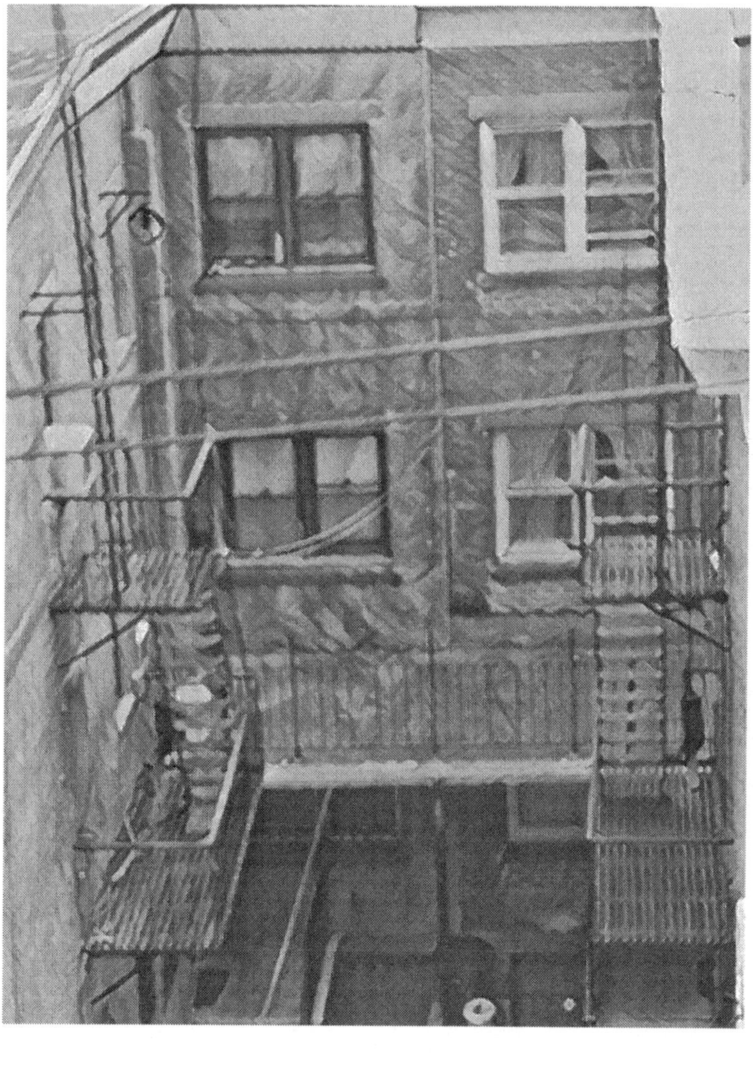

I wanted to set them free for life

because I would only make them dead like me.

They think they took them,

my seeds...

but I gave them to the earth to scatter and to let them breath.

Pollination happens with breezes,

so I hope for winds.

My kids are gusts in my thoughts,

lost in my heart, finding exits in the cracks where pain allows the

breezes to escape.

My love is now a secret garden with many wind chimes.

Listen for the wind catcher's melody,

Bring them back to me.

Inhale

It took me a lifetime to remember. I had given into death.

Breathing now breathes for me;
lungs smuggle in polluted whiffs.

Eyes swollen, now preferring darkness.
My eyes ache more than my thoughts...

Exhale

I'm not tired enough to care, but too tired to walk back into life.

I breathe in memories of a darkened
corner somewhere from my death.

Waiting for life to reclaim me; but it just swallowed me whole,
again.

Breathing

I want my feet to be grounded.
I want my roots reclaimed.
I want to breathe life
again.

The Ashes

I lay on the ground to smell the ashes,
to roll in the cleansing of the blackness.

Earth cleanses, ashes renew, fields lay barren, residue from burnt out flames ignite and allow life to be reclaimed.

I lay on the ground to feel the ashes, to roll in the cleansing of the blackness…to reclaim my life and start over again.

My heart tells my lungs and brain in a blended symphony through unmeasurable pain...

"Just breathe…"

About the Author

Ameerah is a teacher and graduate of New York Institute of Technology, Bloomfield College and University of Phoenix - Phoenix, AZ. She has facilitated poetry programs for middle school, written, produced and directed student productions of Spoken Word and published over 300 student authors/illustrators in that capacity.

She has hosted local poetry venues and currently facilitates an all-Womens' platform, *When Women Speak*. A venue committed to empowering and assisting women in finding their own spiritual, poetic voices.

Ameerah is a photographer with a unique talent of telling stories through poetry and Visual Arts with work exhibited in venues in north and central Jersey.

Her mantra is: "Poetry isn't poetry unless it's Spoken...Word".